I0017794

Guide on iOS 18

Full details of the software
updates and impact to the
Apple ecosystem

By

Barbs Walters

Copyright © 2024, by Barbs Walters.

All rights reserved. No part of this book may be reproduced or transmitted in any form or by any means, electronic or mechanical, including photocopying, recording, or any information storage and retrieval system, without permission in writing from the copyright owner, except for brief quotations in critical reviews and articles.

Table Of Contents

Chapter 1: Introduction to iOS 18

Overview of iOS 18

Apple's iOS 18 is poised to revolutionize the user experience with significant advancements and new features that promise to make the iPhone more customizable and user-friendly than ever before. This latest iteration of Apple's mobile operating system will bring substantial changes, including enhanced customization options, advanced AI integration, and various performance improvements. These updates will be designed not only to meet the evolving needs of iPhone users but also to keep Apple at the forefront of mobile technology.

A New Level of Customization

One of the standout features of iOS 18 will be the extensive customization capabilities for the home screen. Users will have the ability to change the color of app icons and arrange them in any pattern they desire, departing from the traditional grid system that has been in place since the iPhone's inception in 2007. This level of personalization will allow for a truly unique user experience, enabling individuals to tailor their iPhone's appearance to match their preferences and style.

For example, users will be able to group all their social media apps together and assign them a distinct color, such as blue, to easily distinguish them from other app categories like finance or productivity. This feature will not only enhance the aesthetic appeal of the home screen but also improve functionality by making it easier to locate and access frequently used apps.

AI Integration and Custom Emojis

Another major highlight of iOS 18 will be the integration of advanced artificial intelligence (AI) features, particularly in the realm of emojis. Apple will introduce AI-generated emojis, a groundbreaking feature that will create custom emojis on the fly based on the context of the user's text. This means that users will have an endless supply of unique emojis tailored to their specific conversations, significantly enriching the messaging experience.

Imagine texting a friend about a recent vacation and having the AI generate a custom emoji depicting a beach scene, complete with palm trees and waves. This feature will ensure that users always have the perfect emoji to express their thoughts and emotions, reducing the reliance on the existing, often limited, emoji catalog.

Keynote Highlights from June 10

The unveiling of iOS 18 will take place during Apple's annual Worldwide

Developers Conference (WWDC) on June 10. This event is highly anticipated each year, as it provides a platform for Apple to showcase its latest innovations and updates. The keynote presentation, delivered by Apple CEO Tim Cook and other senior executives, will highlight several key aspects of iOS 18.

1. Emphasis on Customization

The keynote will kick off with an in-depth look at the new customization features of iOS 18. Apple's Senior Vice President of Software Engineering, Craig Federighi, will demonstrate the ease with which users can personalize their home screens. By simply tapping and holding on an app icon, users will access a menu that allows them to change the icon's color and move it to any location on the screen. This new functionality will be met with enthusiastic applause from the audience, underscoring the excitement surrounding this long-awaited feature.

2. AI-Powered Enhancements

Next, the focus will shift to the AI-powered enhancements that are set to redefine how users interact with their iPhones. Federighi will showcase the AI-generated emojis, explaining how the system uses advanced machine learning algorithms to understand the context of messages and create relevant emojis in real-time. This demonstration will include several live examples, illustrating the versatility and creativity of the AI in generating a wide array of custom emojis.

3. Improved Performance and Efficiency

In addition to the new features, the keynote will also highlight the performance improvements brought by iOS 18. Apple's Chief Operating Officer, Jeff Williams, will detail how the new operating system optimizes speed and efficiency, resulting in faster app launches and smoother multitasking. He will also mention enhancements to battery life, ensuring that iPhones running iOS 18 will last longer on a single charge, even with the added functionalities.

4. Enhanced Security and Privacy

Apple has always prioritized user privacy, and iOS 18 will continue this tradition with several new security features. Federighi will discuss the introduction of more robust privacy settings, giving users greater control over their data. One notable feature will be the ability to grant apps access to specific photos or files, rather than the entire photo library or file system. This granular control will ensure that users can protect their sensitive information more effectively.

5. Compatibility and Rollout

The keynote will conclude with information on the compatibility of iOS 18. It will be announced that the new operating system will be available for a wide range of iPhone models, from the latest iPhone 16 series to older models like the iPhone 12. This broad compatibility will ensure that a large number of users can benefit from the new features and improvements. The rollout will begin in the fall, with a beta version available to developers immediately and a public beta following shortly after.

6. Focus on AI and Machine Learning

One of the most exciting aspects of iOS 18 will be its focus on AI and machine learning. The keynote will highlight how these technologies are being leveraged to create more intelligent and responsive features. For instance, the AI-generated emojis will be just one example of how machine learning can enhance user interactions.

Additionally, improvements to Siri, Apple's virtual assistant, will be showcased, demonstrating how AI can make Siri more intuitive and helpful in everyday tasks.

7. Expanded Widget Functionality

Federighi will also introduce expanded widget functionality in iOS 18. Widgets, which provide quick access to app information and functions, will be revamped to offer more customization options and better integration with the home screen. Users will be able to resize widgets, choose from a wider variety of designs, and place them anywhere on their home screen. This increased flexibility will make it easier to tailor the iPhone experience to individual needs and preferences.

8. Developer Opportunities

Finally, the keynote will emphasize the opportunities that iOS 18 will present for developers. With new APIs and tools, developers will be able to create more powerful and innovative apps that take full advantage of the new features. Apple will announce several workshops and resources to help developers get up to speed with iOS 18, ensuring that the app ecosystem continues to thrive and expand.

Chapter 2: Customization Features

Customizable App Icons

One of the most exciting aspects of iOS 18 will be the introduction of customizable app icons. This feature will allow users to change the color and appearance of app icons, offering a level of personalization that has never been available on iPhones before.

Changing App Icon Colors

In iOS 18, users will be able to change the colors of their app icons. This means you can make all your social media apps one color, say blue, and your financial apps another color, like green. This ability to color-code your apps will make it easier to find what you're looking for quickly. For example, you will know at a glance that all the green icons are related to your finances, saving you time and making your home screen more organized.

To change an app icon's color, you will just need to tap and hold the icon until a menu appears. From this menu, you will select the "Edit" option and choose your preferred color from a palette. This simple process will give you the freedom to make your home screen truly unique.

Using Custom Icons

In addition to changing colors, iOS 18 will let users replace standard app icons with custom designs. This feature will be great for people who want to give their home screens a specific look or theme. For instance, if you are a fan of minimalistic design, you will be able to use simple, monochrome icons. Alternatively, if you prefer something more vibrant, you can use colorful, detailed icons.

Custom icons can be downloaded from the App Store or created using various graphic design apps. Once you have your custom icons, you will apply them by following a similar process to changing icon colors. This flexibility will make it possible for every iPhone to look different, reflecting the personality and style of its owner.

The Impact on User Experience

Customizable app icons will enhance the user experience in several ways. First, they will make the home screen more visually appealing. With the ability to choose colors and designs, users will enjoy looking at their iPhones even more. Second, it will improve functionality. Color-coding and custom designs will make it easier to find and use apps, especially for people who have many apps installed.

Overall, the introduction of customizable app icons in iOS 18 will provide a significant upgrade to how users interact with their iPhones, making the devices more enjoyable and efficient to use.

Freeform App Placement

Another major customization feature coming with iOS 18 will be the ability to place app icons freely on the home screen. This means users will no longer be restricted to the traditional grid layout that has been a part of iOS since its launch. Instead, you will have the freedom to arrange your apps in any pattern you like.

Breaking Away from the Grid

Currently, iPhone users must place their app icons in a fixed grid pattern. While this layout is clean and orderly, it can feel limiting. With iOS 18, Apple will allow users to break free from this grid. You will be able to drag and drop app icons anywhere on the screen, creating layouts that suit your preferences and needs.

For example, you might decide to place your most-used apps in a circular pattern in the center of the screen for quick access. Alternatively, you could create a more spaced-out layout, leaving gaps between icons for a less cluttered appearance. The possibilities will be endless, giving you full control over your home screen's design.

Grouping and Organizing Apps

Freeform app placement will also make it easier to group and organize apps. With the freedom to move icons anywhere, you will be able to create clusters of related apps. For instance, you could place all your work-related apps in one corner of the screen and your entertainment apps in another. This kind of organization will make it simpler to find and use your apps, enhancing overall efficiency.

Additionally, you will be able to leave entire sections of the home screen empty if you prefer a minimalist look. For example, you might choose to keep only a few essential apps on the main screen, with the rest stored in folders or on additional screens. This flexibility will allow you to design a home screen that matches your unique workflow and style.

Creative and Fun Layouts

The ability to place app icons freely will open up opportunities for creative and fun layouts. You could arrange your apps to form shapes or patterns, such as a smiley face or your initials. This playful approach to home screen design will make using your iPhone more enjoyable.

Moreover, you will be able to change your layout as often as you like. If you get tired of one design, you can easily rearrange your icons to create a new look. This dynamic customization will keep your home screen feeling fresh and interesting over time.

Enhancing Accessibility

Freeform app placement will not only be about aesthetics; it will also improve accessibility. Users with visual impairments or motor skill challenges will benefit from the ability to place apps in locations that are easier for them to see and reach. For instance, you could move essential apps to the bottom of the screen where they are within easier reach of your thumb. This feature will make iPhones more user-friendly for everyone, regardless of their physical abilities.

Implementing Freeform Placement

To use freeform app placement, you will tap and hold an app icon until it starts to wiggle. Then, you will drag the icon to your desired location on the screen. Other icons will move aside to make space, allowing you to create your ideal layout. You will be able to save your layout by pressing the "Done" button, locking the icons in place.

The Future of Home Screen Design

The introduction of freeform app placement in iOS 18 will mark a significant shift in how users interact with their iPhones. This feature will transform the home screen from a static, grid-based layout into a dynamic, customizable space. Users will enjoy the freedom to create layouts that reflect their personalities and meet their needs.

By combining customizable app icons with freeform placement, iOS 18 will offer an unprecedented level of personalization. Whether you want a highly organized, functional home screen or a creative, playful design, you will have the tools to make it happen. This level of customization will make the iPhone feel more like a personal device, tailored to each user's preferences and lifestyle.

Chapter 3: AI Integration

AI-Generated Emojis

One of the most anticipated features in iOS 18 will be AI-generated emojis. This innovative feature will bring a new level of expression and fun to messaging. By using advanced artificial intelligence, iOS 18 will be able to create custom emojis based on what you are typing in real-time. This means that your conversations will become more dynamic and personalized than ever before.

How AI-Generated Emojis Will Work

When you type a message, the AI in iOS 18 will analyze the context and content of your text. Based on this analysis, it will generate unique emojis that match what you are saying. For example, if you are talking about a recent vacation to the beach, the AI might create an emoji with a beach scene, complete with waves and palm trees. This process will happen instantly, allowing you to choose from these custom emojis as you type.

To access these AI-generated emojis, you will simply need to start typing your message. As you type, the AI will suggest emojis that it has created, and you can insert them into your message with a single tap. This seamless integration will make it easy to enhance your texts with unique and relevant emojis.

Personalization and Variety

AI-generated emojis will provide a level of personalization that standard emojis cannot match. Because the AI will create these emojis based on your specific conversations, you will always have the perfect emoji for any situation. This feature will eliminate the frustration of searching through the existing emoji catalog and settling for something that doesn't quite capture what you want to express.

Moreover, the variety of emojis available will be virtually limitless. Since the AI will generate new emojis on the fly, you will not be restricted to a fixed set of options. This means you will always have fresh and interesting emojis to use, keeping your conversations lively and engaging.

Enhancing Communication

Emojis have become an essential part of modern communication, adding emotional nuance and clarity to text messages. AI-generated emojis will take this to the next level by providing more accurate and contextually relevant options. This will help you convey your feelings and thoughts more effectively, making your messages more impactful and easier to understand.

For instance, if you are texting about a celebration, the AI might create an emoji with party elements like confetti and balloons, perfectly capturing the festive mood. This level of detail will enhance your communication, making your texts more expressive and enjoyable for both you and the recipient.

Advanced AI Capabilities

In addition to AI-generated emojis, iOS 18 will introduce several other advanced AI capabilities that will significantly enhance the user experience. These features will leverage machine learning and artificial intelligence to make your iPhone more intuitive and responsive.

Improved Siri Performance

One of the key areas where AI will make a big difference in iOS 18 is in the performance of Siri, Apple's virtual assistant. Siri will become smarter and more capable, thanks to advanced AI algorithms that enable it to understand and respond to complex queries more effectively.

For example, Siri will be able to handle multi-step requests more efficiently. If you ask Siri to find a restaurant nearby, book a table, and set a reminder for the reservation, it will be able to do all of these tasks seamlessly. This improvement will make Siri a more valuable assistant in your daily life, helping you manage tasks and access information more quickly.

Contextual Awareness

AI in iOS 18 will also bring improved contextual awareness to your iPhone. This means that your device will better understand your habits, preferences, and routines, allowing it to provide more relevant and personalized suggestions.

For instance, if you often use a specific app at a certain time of day, iOS 18 will learn this pattern and suggest the app to you when you are likely to use it. This feature will make your iPhone more intuitive, anticipating your needs and helping you save time.

Enhanced Photo Recognition

Photo recognition will be another area where AI will shine in iOS 18. The Photos app will use advanced machine learning to identify and categorize people, objects, and scenes in your pictures more accurately. This will make it easier for you to organize and search through your photo library.

For example, if you want to find all the pictures you took at the beach, you will simply type "beach" into the search bar, and the AI will quickly find all the relevant photos. This enhanced recognition capability will streamline your photo management, making it simpler to relive your favorite memories.

Smart Replies and Suggestions

AI will also enhance the messaging experience by providing smart replies and suggestions. When you receive a message, iOS 18 will analyze the content and context, offering quick reply options that are relevant to the conversation. These smart replies will save you time by providing convenient, pre-written responses that you can send with a tap.

Additionally, iOS 18 will suggest actions based on your messages. For example, if a friend asks you to meet for lunch, your iPhone might suggest adding the event to your calendar or sharing your location. These intelligent suggestions will make it easier to stay organized and responsive in your communications.

Natural Language Processing

The advancements in AI will also improve natural language processing (NLP) on your iPhone. This means that your device will better understand and interpret your spoken and written language, making interactions with Siri and other AI features more accurate and effective.

For example, when you dictate a message or ask Siri a question, the improved NLP capabilities will ensure that your words are understood correctly, even if you use colloquial language or slang. This improvement will make voice interactions more reliable and enjoyable.

AI in Apps and Services

AI will be integrated into various apps and services across iOS 18, enhancing their functionality and making them more useful. For instance, the Maps app will use AI to provide better route suggestions based on real-time traffic data and your personal driving habits. Similarly, the Music app will use AI to recommend songs and playlists that match your listening preferences.

These AI-driven enhancements will make the apps you use every day smarter and more responsive to your needs. Whether you are navigating a new city or discovering new music, AI will help you get the most out of your iPhone.

Privacy and Security

While AI will bring many new capabilities to iOS 18, Apple will remain committed to protecting user privacy and security. All AI processing will be done on-device whenever possible, ensuring that your personal data stays private and secure. Apple will continue to implement strong encryption and other security measures to safeguard your information.

This commitment to privacy will give you peace of mind, knowing that your data is protected even as you enjoy the benefits of advanced AI features. Apple will strive to balance innovation with privacy, delivering powerful AI capabilities without compromising your security.

Chapter 4: User Interface Changes

New Home Screen Layouts

One of the most exciting updates in iOS 18 will be the new home screen layouts. Apple will introduce a flexible and dynamic approach to how you organize and interact with your apps, making the home screen more functional and visually appealing.

Breaking the Grid

For years, iPhone users have been limited to a grid layout for their app icons. While this system has been simple and orderly, it will feel restrictive to many. iOS 18 will break away from this traditional layout, allowing you to place app icons anywhere on the screen. This means you will no longer be bound to a rigid grid pattern, giving you the freedom to create a home screen that truly reflects your personal style and needs.

Custom Layouts

With iOS 18, you will have the ability to create custom layouts for your home screen. This means you can arrange your apps in patterns or shapes that make sense to you. For example, you might choose to place your most-used apps in a circular pattern in the center of the screen for quick access, or you could create a more spaced-out layout to reduce visual clutter.

Creating these custom layouts will be simple. You will tap and hold an app icon until it starts to wiggle, then drag it to your desired location. Other icons will move aside to make space, allowing you to place each app exactly where you want it. This new flexibility will make it easier to find and use your apps, enhancing the overall user experience.

Themes and Aesthetics

In addition to custom layouts, iOS 18 will introduce new themes and aesthetic options for the home screen. This means you can choose from a variety of themes that change the look and feel of your device. Whether you prefer a minimalist design, a vibrant color scheme, or a nature-inspired theme, there will be options to suit your tastes.

Themes will not only change the background and icon colors but also apply a consistent design language across the entire interface. This will create a cohesive and visually pleasing experience, making your iPhone more enjoyable to use.

Adaptive Layouts

Another exciting feature of the new home screen layouts in iOS 18 will be adaptive layouts. This means that the layout will adjust based on the context and your usage patterns. For instance, if you frequently use certain apps at specific times of day, the home screen might highlight these apps during those times, making them easier to access.

Adaptive layouts will also respond to changes in orientation. When you switch from portrait to landscape mode, the home screen will reconfigure itself to optimize the placement of icons and widgets, ensuring that everything remains easily accessible.

Multi-Page Layouts

iOS 18 will also enhance the multi-page layout capabilities of the home screen. This means you can create multiple home screen pages, each with its own unique layout and theme. For example, you might have one page dedicated to work apps, another for entertainment, and a third for social media. Swiping between these pages will be smooth and intuitive, allowing you to organize your apps in a way that best suits your lifestyle.

Enhanced Widget Options

Widgets will become a more integral part of the iPhone experience in iOS 18, with enhanced options and greater customization capabilities. These improvements will make widgets more useful and visually appealing, helping you access important information and functions at a glance.

Resizable Widgets

One of the most significant changes to widgets in iOS 18 will be the ability to resize them. This means you can choose from a variety of widget sizes to suit your needs and preferences. For example, you might select a large calendar widget to see your entire month at a glance, or opt for a smaller weather widget that provides a quick update without taking up too much space.

Resizing widgets will be simple. You will tap and hold a widget until a menu appears, then choose the "Resize" option. This will allow you to adjust the size and shape of the widget, making it fit perfectly within your custom home screen layout.

Interactive Widgets

In addition to being resizable, widgets in iOS 18 will become interactive. This means you can perform actions directly within the widget, without needing to open the corresponding app. For instance, a music widget might include playback controls, allowing you to play, pause, or skip tracks right from the home screen. Similarly, a messaging widget might display recent messages and allow you to reply without opening the app.

Interactive widgets will make it easier to perform common tasks quickly, enhancing your productivity and making your iPhone more convenient to use.

Customizable Widgets

iOS 18 will also introduce more customizable widgets, allowing you to tailor the information and appearance of each widget to suit your needs. For example, a news widget might let you choose the topics or sources you are interested in, ensuring that you only see relevant headlines. Similarly, a fitness widget might allow you to customize the metrics it displays, such as steps taken, calories burned, or workout progress.

To customize a widget, you will tap and hold it until a menu appears, then select the "Edit" option. This will open a settings menu where you can adjust the widget's content and appearance. This level of customization will make widgets more useful and relevant to your daily life.

Dynamic Widgets

Another exciting feature of widgets in iOS 18 will be their dynamic capabilities. Dynamic widgets will update in real-time, providing you with the latest information at a glance. For instance, a weather widget will display current conditions and forecasts, updating as the weather changes. A stock market widget will show real-time stock prices and market trends, ensuring you always have the latest information.

Dynamic widgets will make it easier to stay informed and up-to-date, without needing to constantly check your apps.

Smart Stack Widgets

iOS 18 will also introduce smart stack widgets, which combine multiple widgets into a single, scrollable stack. This means you can save space on your home screen by grouping related widgets together. For example, you might create a smart stack with a calendar, weather, and news widget, allowing you to quickly access all this information by scrolling through the stack.

Smart stack widgets will be customizable, allowing you to choose which widgets to include and the order in which they appear. This will make it easy to create a home screen that is both functional and aesthetically pleasing.

Context-Aware Widgets

Context-aware widgets will be another innovative feature in iOS 18. These widgets will adapt to your current activity and provide relevant information or shortcuts based on what you are doing. For example, if you are at the gym, a fitness widget might display your workout stats and suggest exercises. If you are at work, a productivity widget might show your calendar and to-do list.

Context-aware widgets will use machine learning to understand your habits and preferences, ensuring that they always provide useful and timely information. This will make your iPhone more intuitive and responsive to your needs.

Integrating Widgets with Apps

In iOS 18, widgets will be more deeply integrated with their corresponding apps. This means that actions performed within a widget will sync seamlessly with the app. For example, if you add an event to your calendar using a widget, it will immediately appear in the Calendar app. Similarly, if you update your to-do list from a widget, the changes will reflect in the Reminders app.

This integration will ensure a smooth and consistent experience, making it easier to manage your tasks and information across different parts of your iPhone.

Creating Custom Widgets

iOS 18 will also provide tools for developers to create custom widgets for their apps. This means that you will see a wider variety of widgets available in the App Store, each offering unique functionality and design. Developers will be able to take advantage of the new widget capabilities, creating innovative and useful widgets that enhance the overall user experience.

As a result, you will have access to a rich ecosystem of widgets, allowing you to further customize your home screen and make your iPhone more tailored to your needs.

Chapter 5: Enhanced Security and Privacy

Improved Privacy Features

As the digital landscape evolves, so do the threats to user privacy. iOS 18 will introduce a range of enhanced privacy features designed to give users more control over their personal data and how it is used. These improvements will ensure that your information remains secure and that you have greater transparency about how your data is handled.

App Privacy Reports

One of the standout privacy features in iOS 18 will be the introduction of detailed App Privacy Reports. These reports will provide users with comprehensive insights into how apps access and use their data. You will be able to see which apps have accessed sensitive information such as your location, microphone, camera, and contacts, and how often these accesses have occurred.

To access these reports, you will navigate to the Privacy settings on your iPhone. Here, you will find a new section dedicated to App Privacy Reports. This section will display detailed logs showing each app's data access activities. By reviewing these reports, you will be able to identify any apps that are accessing more data than necessary, allowing you to make informed decisions about which apps to trust.

Enhanced Tracking Protections

Building on the success of App Tracking Transparency introduced in iOS 14, iOS 18 will further enhance tracking protections. Users will have even more control over how their activities are tracked across apps and websites. Apple will introduce new settings that allow you to block tracking more effectively, ensuring that your online behavior remains private.

When you open an app for the first time after installing iOS 18, you will be prompted to choose whether you want to allow tracking. This prompt will be more detailed, providing clear explanations of what tracking entails and how it impacts your privacy. If you choose to deny tracking, the app will not be able to collect or share your data with third parties for advertising or analytics purposes.

Mail Privacy Protection

iOS 18 will also introduce Mail Privacy Protection, a feature designed to protect your email activity from being tracked. When you receive an email, it often contains hidden tracking pixels that can report back to the sender about when and where you opened the email. This information can be used to build a profile of your behavior and preferences.

With Mail Privacy Protection, these tracking pixels will be blocked by default. This means that senders will not be able to see when you opened an email or your location. This feature will help you maintain your privacy while using email, ensuring that your reading habits remain confidential.

Privacy Nutrition Labels

Another important privacy feature in iOS 18 will be the expansion of Privacy Nutrition Labels. These labels, which were introduced in iOS 14, provide users with a clear and concise summary of an app's data practices. In iOS 18, these labels will become even more detailed and easier to understand.

When you visit the App Store, you will see an updated Privacy Nutrition Label for each app. This label will include information about what data the app collects, how it is used, and whether it is shared with third parties. The labels will also indicate whether the app complies with Apple's strict privacy guidelines. This transparency will help you make more informed decisions about which apps to download and use.

Location Privacy Enhancements

Location privacy will also see significant improvements in iOS 18. Apple will introduce new features that give you more control over how and when your location data is shared with apps. You will have the option to provide apps with an approximate location instead of your exact location, reducing the risk of your precise whereabouts being tracked.

Additionally, iOS 18 will introduce a new setting that allows you to grant location access to an app only once. This one-time permission will ensure that the app can access your location only when you explicitly allow it, preventing continuous tracking. If the app needs your location again, it will need to request permission anew.

New Security Measures

In addition to enhancing privacy, iOS 18 will introduce several new security measures designed to protect your device and data from malicious attacks. These measures will leverage advanced technologies to safeguard your iPhone and provide you with peace of mind.

Advanced Face ID and Touch ID

One of the key security enhancements in iOS 18 will be improvements to Face ID and Touch ID. These biometric authentication methods will become more accurate and reliable, ensuring that only you can access your device and sensitive information.

Face ID will benefit from advanced machine learning algorithms that improve its ability to recognize your face in various lighting conditions and angles. This means that Face

ID will work more consistently, even when you are wearing accessories like glasses or hats. Similarly, Touch ID will see improvements in fingerprint recognition accuracy, making it more secure and user-friendly.

On-Device Processing

iOS 18 will continue Apple's commitment to on-device processing, ensuring that sensitive data is processed locally on your iPhone rather than being sent to external servers. This approach enhances security by keeping your data under your control and reducing the risk of it being intercepted or misused.

For example, Siri requests and other personal data will be processed on-device whenever possible. This means that your voice recordings and other sensitive information will not leave your iPhone, maintaining your privacy and security.

Enhanced Data Encryption

Data encryption will be another area of focus in iOS 18. Apple will implement stronger encryption protocols to protect your data both at rest and in transit. This means that your data will be encrypted when it is stored on your device and when it is being transmitted over the internet.

With these enhanced encryption measures, even if your data is intercepted by malicious actors, it will be unreadable and unusable without the decryption key. This will provide an additional layer of security, ensuring that your personal information remains confidential.

Security Audits and Updates

To stay ahead of emerging threats, iOS 18 will include mechanisms for regular security audits and updates. Apple will conduct continuous security assessments of the operating system and its components, identifying and addressing vulnerabilities proactively.

When a security update is available, it will be delivered to your device seamlessly and promptly. These updates will ensure that your iPhone remains protected against the latest threats, providing you with a secure and up-to-date operating environment.

Enhanced App Sandbox

The app sandbox will be another critical security feature in iOS 18. Each app on your iPhone will operate within its own sandboxed environment, isolating it from other apps and the operating system. This isolation will prevent malicious apps from accessing or interfering with your data and system resources.

iOS 18 will introduce enhancements to the app sandbox, further strengthening this isolation. These improvements will make it more difficult for malicious apps to exploit vulnerabilities or gain unauthorized access to your device. As a result, your iPhone will be more resilient against malware and other security threats.

Secure Boot Process

The secure boot process will be another key security measure in iOS 18. This process ensures that your iPhone boots up using only trusted and verified software. When you turn on your device, the boot process will verify the integrity of the operating system and other critical components, ensuring that they have not been tampered with or compromised.

If any issues are detected during the boot process, your iPhone will enter a secure state, preventing it from running potentially malicious software. This will protect your device from boot-level attacks and ensure that it operates securely from the moment it is powered on.

User Education and Awareness

In addition to technical measures, iOS 18 will include features designed to educate users about security best practices and potential threats. Apple will provide resources and prompts to help you understand how to protect your device and data effectively.

For example, iOS 18 will include security tips and guidelines in the Settings app, offering advice on topics such as password management, app permissions, and safe browsing. These resources will empower you to take proactive steps to enhance your security and protect your personal information.

Parental Controls and Family Sharing

iOS 18 will also introduce new features to help parents protect their children's privacy and security. Enhanced parental controls will allow parents to set more granular restrictions on app usage, screen time, and content access. These controls will ensure that children use their devices safely and responsibly.

Family Sharing will also see improvements, allowing families to share purchases, subscriptions, and other content securely. Parents will have more control over what their children can access, and family members will benefit from shared security settings and protections.

Chapter 6: Performance Improvements

Speed and Efficiency Enhancements

With iOS 18, Apple will focus on making significant improvements to the speed and efficiency of iPhones. These enhancements will ensure that your device operates smoothly and responds quickly to your commands, offering a seamless user experience.

Optimized System Processes

One of the key areas of improvement in iOS 18 will be the optimization of system processes. Apple will refine the core operations of the operating system, reducing the time it takes for various tasks to execute. This means that apps will launch faster, system animations will be smoother, and overall responsiveness will be improved.

For example, when you open an app, the system will prioritize the resources needed to launch it quickly. Similarly, multitasking will become more efficient, allowing you to switch between apps without experiencing delays or lag. These optimizations will make everyday interactions with your iPhone more fluid and enjoyable.

Faster App Launch Times

iOS 18 will introduce several under-the-hood enhancements to reduce app launch times. By optimizing how apps are loaded into memory and executed, the operating system will ensure that your favorite apps start up quickly, even if they are resource-intensive.

To achieve this, Apple will implement advanced preloading techniques. This means that the system will anticipate which apps you are likely to use next and prepare them in the background, reducing the time it takes for them to launch when you tap their icons. As a result, you will experience faster access to the apps you use most frequently.

Reduced App Loading Times

In addition to faster app launches, iOS 18 will also reduce the loading times for content within apps. Whether you are browsing the web, loading images, or streaming videos, the system will optimize how data is fetched and rendered, ensuring that content appears more quickly and smoothly.

For example, Safari will benefit from improved data caching and prefetching mechanisms. This means that web pages will load faster, with images and other elements appearing almost instantly. These enhancements will make browsing the internet a more pleasant and efficient experience.

Improved Multitasking

Multitasking will see significant improvements in iOS 18, making it easier to run multiple apps simultaneously without sacrificing performance. The system will better manage background tasks and allocate resources more effectively, ensuring that all active apps continue to perform well.

One of the key features will be enhanced memory management. iOS 18 will optimize how memory is allocated and used, preventing apps from consuming excessive resources. This will reduce the likelihood of apps crashing or becoming unresponsive, even when you have many apps open at once.

Smarter Background Processes

Background processes, such as app updates and data synchronization, will become smarter and more efficient in iOS 18. The system will prioritize these tasks based on your usage patterns and network conditions, ensuring that they do not interfere with your active tasks.

For example, iOS 18 will delay non-essential background activities when you are using your device intensively, such as during gaming or video calls. These activities will be scheduled for times when your device is idle or connected to a stable Wi-Fi network, minimizing their impact on performance.

Enhanced Graphics Performance

Graphics performance will also receive a boost in iOS 18. Apple will implement optimizations to the graphics processing unit (GPU), ensuring that games and other graphics-intensive applications run more smoothly and efficiently.

These improvements will be particularly noticeable in high-end games and augmented reality (AR) applications. With enhanced GPU performance, you will experience more realistic graphics, smoother animations, and faster frame rates, making gaming and AR experiences more immersive and enjoyable.

Streamlined System Updates

System updates in iOS 18 will become more streamlined, reducing the time it takes to download and install new versions of the operating system. Apple will optimize the update process, ensuring that updates are applied quickly and with minimal disruption to your device usage.

For instance, iOS 18 will introduce a new update mechanism that downloads only the necessary components, rather than the entire operating system. This will reduce the size of updates and the time required to install them. Additionally, updates will be applied in the background, allowing you to continue using your device without interruption.

Battery Life Optimization

Battery life is a critical aspect of mobile device performance, and iOS 18 will introduce several enhancements to help you get the most out of your iPhone's battery. These optimizations will ensure that your device lasts longer on a single charge, allowing you to stay connected and productive throughout the day.

Intelligent Battery Management

One of the key features of iOS 18 will be intelligent battery management. The operating system will use advanced algorithms to monitor your battery usage and make adjustments to extend battery life. This will involve optimizing how power is allocated to different tasks and apps, ensuring that your battery is used more efficiently.

For example, iOS 18 will identify apps that consume a significant amount of power and suggest actions to reduce their impact. You will receive notifications if an app is running in the background and using a lot of battery, allowing you to take action by closing the app or adjusting its settings.

Adaptive Power Modes

iOS 18 will introduce adaptive power modes that adjust the device's performance based on your usage patterns and battery level. These power modes will help conserve battery life by reducing the performance of non-essential tasks when the battery is low or when you are not actively using your device.

For instance, if your battery is running low, iOS 18 will automatically enter a low power mode, reducing background activity and lowering the screen brightness to conserve energy. This will help extend the battery life, allowing you to continue using your device until you can recharge it.

Enhanced Battery Health Management

Battery health management will be another important focus in iOS 18. The operating system will include new tools and features to help you monitor and maintain the health of your iPhone's battery, ensuring that it remains in good condition over time.

You will be able to access detailed battery health information in the Settings app, including the maximum capacity and peak performance capability of your battery. iOS 18 will also provide recommendations for actions you can take to preserve battery health, such as avoiding extreme temperatures and optimizing charging habits.

Optimized Charging

Optimized charging will be enhanced in iOS 18, further protecting your battery from wear and tear. This feature will learn your charging routine and adjust the charging speed to reduce battery aging. For example, if you regularly charge your iPhone overnight, iOS 18 will slow down the charging process after reaching 80% capacity, completing the charge just before you wake up.

This gradual charging process will reduce the stress on the battery, helping to extend its lifespan. Additionally, iOS 18 will provide notifications and tips to help you optimize your charging habits, ensuring that you get the most out of your battery.

Efficient App Management

Efficient app management will be another key feature in iOS 18, helping to reduce battery consumption by optimizing how apps run in the background. The operating system will use machine learning to identify apps that are not being used frequently and limit their background activity to save power.

For example, iOS 18 will monitor apps that frequently wake up the device or perform unnecessary background tasks. These apps will be placed in a dormant state when not in use, reducing their impact on battery life. You will also receive notifications if an app is consuming a significant amount of battery, allowing you to take action to limit its activity.

Reduced Power Consumption for Display

The display is one of the most power-hungry components of a mobile device, and iOS 18 will introduce several features to reduce its power consumption. These features will help extend battery life by optimizing how the display operates based on your usage patterns and environmental conditions.

For instance, iOS 18 will include an adaptive brightness feature that adjusts the screen brightness based on ambient light levels. This will ensure that the display is not brighter than necessary, reducing power consumption and improving battery life. Additionally, iOS 18 will introduce new display technologies that are more energy-efficient, further reducing the impact of the display on battery life.

Power-Efficient Background Tasks

iOS 18 will optimize how background tasks are handled to reduce their impact on battery life. The operating system will prioritize essential background activities, such as email synchronization and messaging notifications, while minimizing the power consumption of non-essential tasks.

For example, iOS 18 will batch background tasks together, allowing them to be executed more efficiently. This means that tasks like app updates and data synchronization will be performed in groups, reducing the number of times the device needs to wake up and perform background activities. This approach will help conserve battery life while ensuring that essential tasks are still completed in a timely manner.

Energy-Efficient Networking

Networking activities, such as downloading data and syncing with cloud services, can also impact battery life. iOS 18 will introduce new features to make these activities more energy-efficient, helping to extend battery life while maintaining connectivity.

For instance, iOS 18 will include an optimized networking feature that reduces the power consumption of Wi-Fi and cellular data connections. This feature will intelligently manage how data is transmitted and received, ensuring that networking activities are performed efficiently. Additionally, iOS 18 will include new protocols that reduce the power consumption of data-intensive tasks, such as video streaming and large file downloads.

Chapter 7: Compatibility and Device Support

Supported iPhone Models

As Apple prepares to launch iOS 18, one of the most anticipated aspects will be the list of supported iPhone models. Compatibility is crucial because it determines which devices will receive the new features, improvements, and security updates that come with the latest operating system. Apple aims to ensure that as many users as possible can benefit from iOS 18, while also taking into account the technical capabilities of older devices.

Criteria for Compatibility

Apple will use a combination of hardware capabilities and performance metrics to determine which iPhone models are compatible with iOS 18. Devices need to have sufficient processing power, memory, and other hardware specifications to run the new features smoothly. Additionally, Apple will consider user experience, ensuring that the update does not negatively impact the performance of older devices.

Expected Supported Models

Based on trends from previous iOS updates, iOS 18 is expected to support a broad range of iPhone models. Typically, Apple supports devices released within the last five to six years. Given this, the following models are likely to be compatible with iOS 18:

- iPhone 12 Series: iPhone 12, iPhone 12 Mini, iPhone 12 Pro, iPhone 12 Pro Max
- iPhone 13 Series: iPhone 13, iPhone 13 Mini, iPhone 13 Pro, iPhone 13 Pro Max
- iPhone 14 Series: iPhone 14, iPhone 14 Plus, iPhone 14 Pro, iPhone 14 Pro Max
- iPhone 15 Series: iPhone 15, iPhone 15 Plus, iPhone 15 Pro, iPhone 15 Pro Max
- iPhone 16 Series: iPhone 16, iPhone 16 Plus (the latest models to be launched this fall)

Older models like the iPhone 11 series and possibly even the iPhone XR and XS might also be included, depending on their hardware capabilities. However, support for these older models will focus more on security updates and basic features, rather than all the advanced functionalities of iOS 18.

Legacy Support Considerations

While Apple strives to include as many devices as possible, there are limitations to what older hardware can handle. For models that are several years old, Apple will provide a more streamlined version of iOS 18, ensuring that critical security updates and essential features are available without compromising performance.

For example, older devices might not receive advanced AI features or high-end graphical enhancements due to hardware constraints. Apple will prioritize stability and usability for these models, ensuring that they continue to perform well even with the new software.

Phased Feature Rollout

In some cases, Apple might adopt a phased rollout for certain features of iOS 18, especially for older models. This means that while all compatible devices will receive the update, some advanced features might be introduced gradually, starting with the latest models and extending to older ones as performance and compatibility are confirmed.

This approach allows Apple to ensure that all features work optimally on each device, addressing any performance issues or bugs that might arise during the initial rollout. It also helps manage user expectations, ensuring that everyone benefits from the update while maintaining device stability.

Update Rollout Schedule

The rollout schedule for iOS 18 will be carefully planned to ensure a smooth transition for all users. Apple typically follows a predictable update cycle, and iOS 18 will be no different. The schedule will be designed to accommodate different regions, carriers, and device models, ensuring a seamless experience for all iPhone users.

Announcement and Developer Beta

The journey to iOS 18 will begin with its official announcement during Apple's Worldwide Developers Conference (WWDC) on June 10. During this keynote event, Apple will unveil the new features and enhancements of iOS 18, providing an in-depth look at what users can expect.

Following the announcement, Apple will release the first developer beta. This version will be available to registered developers, allowing them to test the new operating system on their devices and update their apps to ensure compatibility with iOS 18. The developer beta phase is crucial for identifying and fixing bugs, optimizing performance, and gathering feedback from the developer community.

Public Beta Program

After a few weeks of developer testing, Apple will launch the public beta program for iOS 18. This program will allow any interested users to try out the new operating system ahead of its official release. To participate, users will need to sign up for the Apple Beta Software Program and install the beta profile on their devices.

The public beta phase will provide Apple with valuable feedback from a broader user base, helping to identify and resolve any remaining issues. It also gives users an opportunity to experience the new features and provide input on their functionality and usability.

Final Release Candidate

As the public beta phase progresses and Apple addresses feedback from both developers and beta testers, the company will release the final release candidate (RC) version of iOS 18. This version will be nearly identical to the official release, with any last-minute tweaks and bug fixes incorporated.

The RC version will be made available to developers and public beta testers, allowing them to ensure that their apps and devices are fully prepared for the official rollout. This phase will typically last for a few weeks, providing a final opportunity to catch and address any critical issues.

Official Release

The official release of iOS 18 will coincide with the launch of the new iPhone 16 series in the fall. Typically, this happens in September. Apple will roll out the update to all compatible devices simultaneously, making it available for download through the Settings app on your iPhone.

To install the update, you will need to go to Settings > General > Software Update and follow the on-screen instructions. The update process will be straightforward, with options to download and install the update automatically or schedule it for a convenient time.

Staggered Rollout

While Apple aims for a simultaneous release, the rollout of iOS 18 might be staggered across different regions and carriers to ensure a smooth transition. This approach helps manage server load and ensures that support teams are available to assist users with any issues that might arise during the update process.

In practice, this means that while most users will receive the update on the official release day, some might see a slight delay of a few days. Apple will provide regular updates on the rollout status, ensuring that users are informed about when they can expect to receive iOS 18.

Post-Release Updates

Following the official release of iOS 18, Apple will continue to provide regular updates to address any bugs, security vulnerabilities, and performance issues that might be discovered. These updates, often referred to as "point releases" (e.g., iOS 18.1, iOS 18.2), will be rolled out periodically to ensure that your device remains secure and performs optimally.

These post-release updates will also introduce minor feature enhancements and improvements based on user feedback.

Apple will use these updates to refine the operating system and ensure that it meets the needs and expectations of its users.

Long-Term Support

Apple is known for providing long-term support for its devices, and iOS 18 will be no exception. Compatible iPhone models will continue to receive updates for several years, ensuring that they remain secure and functional. This long-term support extends the lifespan of your device, allowing you to enjoy the latest features and enhancements without needing to upgrade to a new model immediately.

User Preparation and Education

To help users prepare for the update, Apple will provide comprehensive resources and guidance. This will include detailed information about the new features and how to use them, as well as tips for optimizing your device's performance and battery life after the update.

Apple will also offer support through its various channels, including the Apple Support app, online forums, and customer service centers. This ensures that you have access to assistance if you encounter any issues during or after the update process.

Chapter 8: Future Prospects

Anticipated Updates and Features

As iOS 18 prepares to debut, the future prospects for Apple's operating system look promising. While the initial release will bring a host of new features and improvements, Apple will likely continue to evolve iOS 18 with subsequent updates. These updates will not only refine existing functionalities but also introduce new capabilities that will further enhance the user experience.

Continued AI Integration

One of the key areas where Apple will likely continue to innovate is in artificial intelligence (AI). The introduction of AI-generated emojis in iOS 18 will be just the beginning. Future updates will expand on this, incorporating AI more deeply into various aspects of the operating system.

For instance, Apple will enhance Siri's capabilities, making it smarter and more intuitive. Siri will be able to understand and respond to more complex queries, provide personalized recommendations, and integrate more seamlessly with third-party apps. This will make Siri a more useful and indispensable tool in everyday tasks.

Additionally, AI will improve predictive text and autocorrect features, making typing on your iPhone faster and more accurate. By learning from your typing habits and preferences, AI will suggest words and phrases that are more relevant to you, reducing the time you spend correcting errors.

Enhanced Augmented Reality (AR) Features

Apple has been investing heavily in augmented reality, and future updates to iOS 18 will likely see significant advancements in this area. The company will introduce new AR tools and frameworks that will allow developers to create even more immersive and interactive AR experiences.

For example, iOS 18 will support advanced ARKit features that enable more precise tracking of real-world objects and environments. This will make AR applications, such as games and educational tools, more realistic and engaging. Additionally, new AR features will be integrated into everyday apps, such as Maps and Photos, providing users with useful and entertaining ways to interact with their surroundings.

Expanded Health and Fitness Capabilities

Health and fitness have become a major focus for Apple, and future updates to iOS

18 will likely introduce new features in this domain. The Health app will gain more advanced tracking capabilities, allowing users to monitor a wider range of health metrics and receive personalized insights.

For example, future updates will introduce features that track mental health and wellness, such as mood logging and stress management tools. These features will use data from various sensors and inputs to provide a comprehensive view of your overall health.

Additionally, fitness tracking will become more accurate and versatile, with new workout types and activities being added. Integration with third-party fitness equipment and apps will be improved, allowing for a more seamless and connected fitness experience.

Improved Accessibility Features

Apple will continue to prioritize accessibility, ensuring that iOS 18 is usable by everyone, including those with disabilities. Future updates will introduce new accessibility features that make the operating system more inclusive and easier to navigate.

For instance, voice control and screen reader functionalities will be enhanced, providing more options and customization for users with visual or motor impairments. Additionally, new tools will be introduced to assist users with cognitive disabilities, making it easier to use and understand the various features of iOS 18.

More Customization Options

Customization will remain a key theme in future updates to iOS 18. Apple will introduce new ways for users to personalize their devices, making them truly their own. This will include more options for customizing app icons, widgets, and home screen layouts.

For example, future updates will allow users to create custom themes that change the overall look and feel of their device. This will include options for customizing colors, fonts, and animations, providing a more personalized user experience. Additionally, new widget designs and configurations will be introduced, allowing users to tailor their home screens to better suit their needs and preferences.

Enhanced Privacy and Security Features

Privacy and security will continue to be a top priority for Apple, and future updates to iOS 18 will introduce new measures to protect user data and ensure a secure experience. These updates will include advanced encryption methods, improved data transparency, and new tools for managing app permissions.

For instance, future updates will introduce more granular controls for app permissions, allowing users to specify exactly what data each app can access. Additionally, new features will be introduced to alert users to potential security threats and provide guidance on how to protect their devices and data.

Integration with New Hardware

As Apple continues to innovate with new hardware, future updates to iOS 18 will be designed to take full advantage of these advancements. This will include support for new sensors, cameras, and other technologies that enhance the capabilities of your iPhone.

For example, future updates will introduce features that leverage new camera technologies to improve photography and videography. This will include advanced computational photography techniques that produce higher-quality images and videos, as well as new editing tools that make it easier to create professional-looking content.

Impact on the iPhone Ecosystem

The introduction of iOS 18 and its subsequent updates will have a profound impact on the iPhone ecosystem. These changes will influence how users interact with their devices, how developers create apps, and how the overall mobile landscape evolves.

User Experience

The enhanced features and improvements in iOS 18 will elevate the user experience, making iPhones more powerful and user-friendly. Users will enjoy faster performance, longer battery life, and more customization options, allowing them to tailor their devices to their needs and preferences.

Additionally, the integration of advanced AI and AR capabilities will open up new possibilities for how users interact with their devices. Everyday tasks will become more intuitive and efficient, and new forms of entertainment and productivity will emerge.

Developer Opportunities

For developers, iOS 18 will present new opportunities to create innovative apps and services. The new tools and frameworks introduced in iOS 18 will enable developers to push the boundaries of what is possible, creating more engaging and useful applications.

For example, the enhanced ARKit features will allow developers to create more sophisticated AR experiences, attracting new users and driving engagement. Additionally, the improved AI capabilities will enable developers to build smarter apps that provide personalized experiences and insights.

Ecosystem Growth

The continuous evolution of iOS 18 will contribute to the growth of the iPhone ecosystem. As new features and capabilities are introduced, more users will be drawn to the platform, expanding the user base and creating a larger market for apps and services.

This growth will also drive innovation, as developers and companies seek to capitalize on the new opportunities presented by iOS 18. This will result in a more vibrant and dynamic ecosystem, with a diverse range of apps and services available to users.

Competition and Market Position

The advancements in iOS 18 will help Apple maintain its competitive edge in the mobile market. By continuously improving the operating system and introducing cutting-edge features, Apple will attract new users and retain existing ones, strengthening its market position.

The focus on privacy and security will also differentiate Apple from its competitors, appealing to users who prioritize these aspects. As concerns about data privacy continue to grow, Apple's commitment to protecting user data will be a significant advantage in the market.

Integration with Other Apple Devices

iOS 18 will also enhance the integration between iPhones and other Apple devices, such as iPads, Macs, and Apple Watches.

This seamless integration will create a more cohesive and connected ecosystem, allowing users to easily switch between devices and enjoy a consistent experience.

For example, new features in iOS 18 will enable better synchronization of data and settings across devices, making it easier to start a task on one device and continue it on another. This will enhance productivity and convenience, further strengthening the appeal of the Apple ecosystem.

Long-Term Vision

In the long term, iOS 18 will lay the groundwork for future innovations and developments. The advancements introduced in this update will serve as a foundation for new technologies and features that Apple will continue to develop in the coming years.

For instance, the improvements in AI and AR will pave the way for more sophisticated applications, such as advanced virtual assistants and immersive augmented reality experiences. The focus on customization and personalization will also drive future updates, as Apple continues to empower users to make their devices uniquely their own.

www.ingramcontent.com/pod-product-compliance
Lightning Source LLC
LaVergne TN
LVHW051703050326
832903LV00032B/3975